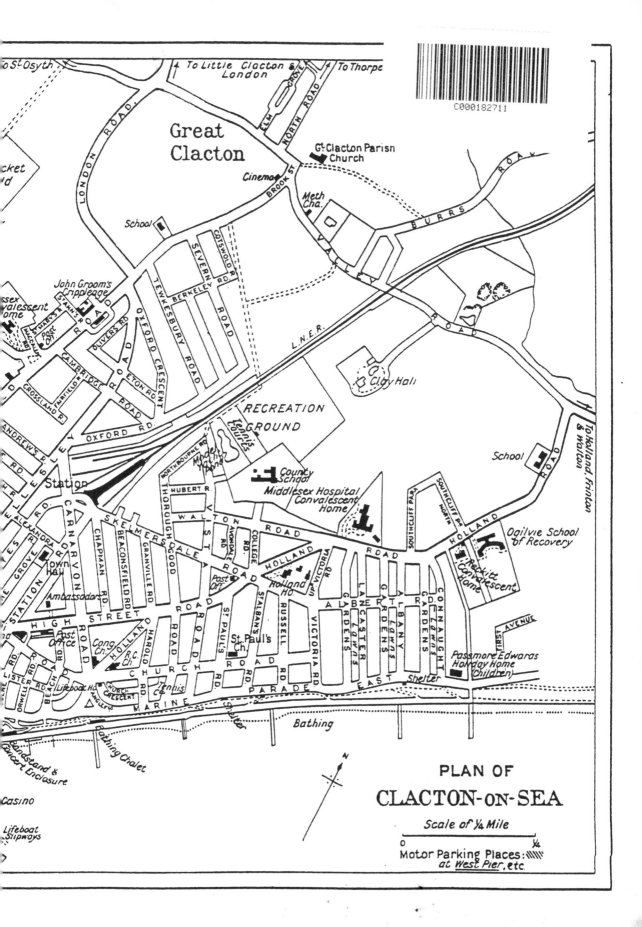

PLAN OF
CLACTON-ON-SEA

Scale of ¼ Mile

Motor Parking Places: ⫸⫸⫸
at West Pier, etc.

CLACTON-ON-SEA
A Pictorial History

Welcome to Clacton ... and the book!

CLACTON-ON-SEA
A Pictorial History

Norman Jacobs

Phillimore

1993

Published by
PHILLIMORE & CO LTD.,
Shopwyke Manor Barn, Chichester, Sussex

ISBN 0 85033 871 9

Printed and bound in Great Britain by
BIDDLES LTD.,
Guildford, Surrey

To Linda

List of Illustrations

Frontispiece: Everything happens at Clacton

Illustration Acknowledgements

The illustrations appear by kind permission of the following: Mrs. G. Agate, 17, 87, 179; Mrs. Cynthia Baker, 180; Mr. Mark Barrett, 96, 157; Mr. K. E. Carrington, 176; Mr. Cattermole, 19, 28, 165, 169; Clacton & District Local History Society, 1, 12, 34, 43, 48, 62, 69, 70, 84, 85, 89, 112, 115, 139, 148, 149, 160, 167; Mr. Brian Essam (of the Fairclough family), 18, 79, 171; Essex County Cricket Club, 150; Mrs. Linda Fitch, 55, 56, 73, 75, 147, 174; Mrs. Lorna Gillespie, 173, 175; Mrs. Gosling, 152, 177; Mr. George Hardwick, 65, 71, 118, 156; Mr. Roy Hudd, 116; Mr. A. Johnson, 54; Mr. Peter Kingsman, 61, 90, 91, 95, 97, 98, 100-102, 108, 154; Mrs. P. Manser, 51; Mrs. Rhodes, 26; Mr. Cliff Richard, 117; Miss Vi Stewart, 29; Tendring District Council, frontispiece, 7, 8, 15, 16, 20, 39, 40, 59, 64, 72, 86, 88, 103-105, 110, 111, 119, 121-126, 129, 137, 138, 141-146, 151, 153, 162, 168; Mrs. Barbara Wright, 45-47, 130, 163; Messrs. Bob and Reg Young, 113; Mr. Reg Young, 78. All other illustrations are from the author's own collection.

Acknowledgements

As well as the owners of original photographs acknowledged separately, I would like to thank the following for the time and support they have given me in the preparation of this book: Kenneth Walker, author of *The History of Clacton*; Frank Black, Roger Kennell and Peter Palmer of the Clacton & District Local History Society; the staff at Tendring District Council, in particular John Margerum, Andrew Mowle and Bob Foster; Barbara Winter and Alan Lacey for their help with the photography; Sandra Mooney for help with typing the manuscript; the staff of Clacton Library and last, but by no means least, my family, Linda, Robert, Tom, Nanny and Grandad, for putting up with my obsession with Clacton.

Introduction

Clacton-on-Sea is a seaside resort situated on the Essex coast about eighty miles north-east of London. It is in the curious position of being one of the oldest known sites of human habitation in Great Britain and yet, at the same time, a comparatively new town.

In common with much of Essex, the Clacton soil consists mainly of London clay capped by valley gravels, which is exposed on the cliff-face. Nodules of argillaceous limestone or septaria, used by the Romans in making cement, are present in the cliffs. The sheets of valley gravel have yielded many interesting fossil remains in and around Clacton, from rare molluscs to large mammals such as the woolly rhinoceros, mammoth, cave-lion and straight-tusked elephant. At the time when such mammals roamed the area, Great Britain was still connected to the continent of Europe, and it was at the place we now know as Clacton-on-Sea that a band of wandering people set up camp on the banks of the River Thames, which at that time flowed on a more northerly course linking up with the Rhine. Their settlement dates from something like 420,000 years ago, just as the climate was warming up following the Anglian glacial period and as Europe was entering the Hoxnian inter-glacial period.

No remains in the form of human bones have ever been found but literally thousands of flint implements have been discovered in an area stretching from Tower Road along the cliffs and shore-line to Jaywick. An important artefact left by these old stone-age people was discovered in 1911 by an amateur archaeologist, J. Hazzledine Warren, when he came across the end of a wooden spear sticking out of the cliffs below what is now Clacton hospital. This spear, dating back some 250,000 years, is the oldest known man-made wooden artefact found anywhere in the world.

In about 5000 B.C., the new stone-age people also set up camp in the same area. By this time Great Britain had separated from Europe and Clacton's long battle against erosion had begun. The new stone-age settlement is now almost completely covered by the sea and remains of this neolithic village are all but lost beneath the waves. Erosion and landslips have been the pattern of this part of the coast ever since and even as late as the turn of this century it was calculated that at Little Holland (now Holland-on-Sea) on one mile of frontage three acres of land were being lost every eight years.

Eventually it was the Celtic people (the Catuvellauni) in the last century B.C. who moved Clacton about a mile inland and set up a farming community in a small forest clearing, the site of which was later to become, under the Saxons, the village still known today as Great Clacton. The name is, in fact, derived from three Saxon words: Clacc-inga-ton – the village of Clacc's people, Clacc being the name of the local chief.

At the time of Domesday Book (1086) it was recorded that 'Clachintuna' was populated by 45 tenant farmers and 50 smallholders and was part of a manor belonging to the Bishops of London. In 1108 Richard de Belmeis was appointed Bishop of London and he must have been responsible for founding the present parish church of St John the Baptist, as parts of the nave date back to this period.

For much of Great Clacton's history as an independent parish the church was at the centre of village life, religious of course, but also temporal. Probably its most famous incumbent was the Rev. Eleazar Knox, second son of the great Scottish reformer John Knox. Eleazar Knox was vicar from 1587 to 1591. As the centre of local government, the church hosted the village elders' annual vestry meeting, from which the parish affairs were controlled. Held every Easter, this meeting set the rates for the forthcoming year and appointed the parish officers including two churchwardens and two surveyors, whose job it was to maintain the village streets.

Great Clacton's other major annual event was the Midsummer Fair, held every year on 29 June. The fair filled up St John's Square and spread along The Street (now St John's Road) enveloping practically the whole of the village with swings, stalls, sideshows, showmen and pedlars of every description. Beginning in the 12th century, the fair was finally abolished in 1872.

The whole of the village's *official* economy was centred on agriculture, the chief crops being wheat, oats and barley, with most of the villagers being employed as farm labourers. However, proximity to the sea meant that there was also a large *unofficial* economy as many of the villagers were involved, one way or another, with smuggling; the lonely beach was ideal for, and rife with, this activity, which reached its height in the 18th century. In 1728 for example, a reward was offered for the apprehension of a gang of thirty or forty smugglers, while several years later another gang of 17 smugglers was caught by customs officers, who were themselves captured by yet another gang!

Great Clacton's proximity to the beach was also responsible for its close involvement in Britain's defence against a possible invasion by Napoleon in the late 18th and early 19th centuries. It was considered by the War Office that the most likely spot for an enemy landing lay between Walton Gap and Clacton Wick (Wash Lane). Consequently, this area was heavily fortified with three martello towers built close together near Clacton Wick.

However, due to Clacton Beach's ill-deserved reputation at the time of suffering from 'noxious vapours' (as the Colchester historian Philip Morant had complained), the soldiers manning the towers were actually stationed several miles inland at Weeley Barracks. Their daily tramp to and from the beach took them through Great Clacton. This great influx of visitors brought undreamt-of prosperity to the village. For example, the owner of the *Queen's Head Inn* was able to build the large two-storey bow-fronted addition facing on to St John's Road; the upstairs was used as a ballroom by the officers. The soldiers created other disturbances, as it was reported that the Cameron Highlanders shocked the ladies by wearing kilts and revealing their bare knees!

Dependence on agriculture led directly to the village's last great upheaval before the coming of the seaside town when, on 7 December 1830, a crowd of farm workers surged into The Street with the intention of visiting the local farms and smashing their machinery, which they considered to be responsible for lowering their wages and putting many of them out of work. The riot lasted for several days before a force of nearly one thousand farmers and local gentry was able to stop it. Many of the rioters were arrested and at least three transported for seven years.

It was during this period, in the early and mid-19th century, that seaside holidays started to become popular and a number of people eyed the sandy shore of Clacton Beach with a view to developing the area as a resort. In 1824, for example, the proprietor of the *Ship Inn* at Great Clacton was advertising a bathing machine available for hire on Clacton Beach; in about 1830 a Colchester developer, named Sargent Lay, made enquiries about the area in the hope of developing a seaside resort.

For the time being, however, it was not to be. The land belonged to a farm called Sea Side House Farm (situated on the corner of what is now Station Road and Rosemary Road) which was held in trust in the names of Mr. and Mrs. William Watson, thus preventing any prospective purchasers from buying up the land and developing it.

In 1864 this trust expired with the death of William Watson. The land was divided into lots and put up for auction by the estate's executors. Before the sale could take place, however, the land was bought in one lot by private treaty by a man called Peter Bruff.

At the time Bruff was the engineer on the Colchester-Walton railway, having already masterminded the Shoreditch-Colchester line and the Colchester-Ipswich track. He also had extensive interests in Colchester, Walton, Felixstowe, Harwich and Ipswich and was a typical example of the Victorian industrial entrepreneur, ready to turn his hand to anything connected with engineering.

Bruff bought the land belonging to Sea Side House Farm with the sole intention of turning the area into a seaside resort. In 1866 he sought, and was granted, powers by Parliament to extend his railway to Clacton-on-Sea, with a new station just 50 yards from the cliffs, and to build a pier so that paddle steamers could visit his new resort. The powers were granted for a period of five years after which time they would lapse. Unfortunately, just at the time he needed it, Bruff's capital was tied up in other projects and he was unable to make a start on his new town. In fact, Bruff was unable to do anything until the middle of 1870, just one year before his powers were due to expire. It was then that he arranged a meeting with a man called William Parry Jackson, the chairman of the Woolwich Steam Packet Co., which operated paddle steamers from London to the East Coast.

The meeting took place on a desolate Clacton beach. It is hard to imagine what it must have been like. We are now used to seeing the beach with its landscaped cliff gardens, the zig-zag paths and the concrete promenade, a few shops above the beach, the busy town just beyond the Venetian Bridge, the glass-fronted Pavilion to the east of the pier and, of course, the pier itself jutting out into the sea with its many buildings and fairground rides. But on that portentous day in July 1870, there was none of this – only the rough sea and the windswept sand, grass and weeds of a lonely beach with just the bare gaunt cliffs behind to serve as a bleak and barren backdrop to the vision of those two men, Bruff and Jackson. At this fateful meeting, Jackson agreed to finance Bruff's scheme in return for the right to make Clacton an exclusive port of call for his paddle steamers.

So on 18 July 1871, just as the five-year deadline was about to be reached, the first building in the new town of Clacton-on-Sea, the pier, was finished and the steamer *Queen of the Orwell* called on its way to Ipswich. The following week saw the official opening of the pier when, on 27 July, the SS *Albert Edward* brought a party of directors from the Woolwich Steam Packet Co. and about two hundred guests to the new resort. After the official opening ceremony the visitors were able to spend a few hours on the beach. There was great excitement when one couple arrived back at the pier to find the *Albert Edward* already leaving. They quickly managed to obtain a small boat to take them out. Unfortunately, on trying to transfer, the lady fell overboard. She was fished out of the sea very wet but otherwise unharmed. A symbolic 'baptism' for the new town!

With the pier a reality, and with the financial backing of the Woolwich Steam Packet Co. assured, Peter Bruff and the company's directors turned their attention to attracting visitors to their newly created watering place. A couple of projects followed: firstly, the *Royal Hotel* opened on 24 July 1872, and then the Public Hall in Pier Avenue in 1877. Meanwhile, plots of land were being sold off to individual developers by Peter Bruff, who had laid down strict conditions, known as his 'Deed of Mutual Covenants', by which all purchasers had to abide. These covenants covered matters such as fencing, drainage, paving and lighting. Bruff was also responsible for the road layout of the new town and to all intents and purposes had become a one-man town planning department. It is largely thanks to him that the centre of Clacton still retains that airy and well-laid out feel with wide streets and well-spaced shops and houses which remains to this day.

Early building was concentrated along Pier Avenue, Pallister Road, Rosemary Road and Marine Parade, as far as Colne Road and Orwell Road to the east, and Agate Road to the west. Gradually more and more land was acquired for development as other local landowners, notably H. J. Page to the east and James Round to the west, also laid out parts of their estates. By the mid-1880s Clacton had already become a busy seaside resort.

Bruff's original intention for *his* seaside town was that it should become a high-class resort catering for an exclusive middle- and upper-class clientèle. However, as the town grew, especially after the railway eventually arrived in 1882, more and more day trippers and excursionists were being attracted. The newer shopkeepers, hotel owners and café proprietors were delighted with this state of affairs, but the old guard – the original pioneers – viewed this new development with some suspicion, not to say horror! For whilst they recognised that the influx of visitors was good for business they were concerned that works outings and other similar excursions were lowering the tone of the place. In 1884, for example, a complaint was made about 'riotous and reckless excursionists'. The complaint warned:

Clacton-on-Sea will soon have a painful and even ruinous experience if speedy measures be not taken to stop the present rush of the lowest type of London excursionists – men and women, boys and girls – who seem only to enjoy themselves when they are revelling in drink and obscenity, both of language and behaviour.

The symbolic epitome of this conflict between the upper-class proponents and the popular resort proponents came in 1885 when two planning proposals were put forward – one to build a mansion on Marine Parade and the other to build a urinal in Pier Avenue. Mansion or urinal seemed to sum up Clacton's dilemma of the 1880s. With the subsequent victory of the urinal over the mansion Clacton's fate was sealed. The Minstrel shows, German bands, donkey rides and shellfish stalls took over from the public lectures, the circulating libraries and the quiet reading rooms.

Clacton's image may have changed between the 1880s and '90s but its rapid growth continued unabated. The census of 1881 showed a total population of 651. By

1901 this number had reached 7,456. Its summer visitors also increased rapidly, as can be seen by just one statistic: in 1883, 92,873 people paid to promenade on the pier; by 1893 this figure had rocketed to a staggering 327,451.

While all these changes had been taking place at the seaside, the older families and village elders at Great Clacton had looked askance at the newcomers and their activities and, for the most part, decided that they wished to have nothing to do with them. One or two of the more progressive thinkers, like Henry Finer, who lived in St John's House by the churchyard, did recognise the potential for business in the new town, but, on the whole, most were content to continue life as before.

A sign of the changing times, however, came with the result of Clacton's first election. This took place in 1884 when a new Parochial Committee was formed comprising both Great Clacton and the new town. There were 11 candidates for seven positions. All but one of the seven elected were from the new Clacton-on-Sea business community, whilst every single one of the four defeated candidates was from the older Great Clacton families.

As the long Victorian age finally gave way to the Edwardian era the popular image of the friendly and bustling seaside town that Clacton-on-Sea was to conjure up in the minds of millions of visitors throughout the 20th century had become firmly established. It had eclipsed the elders of the ancient village and it had seen off Peter Bruff's plans to turn it into a select high-class resort. By the early years of the century there were three shows operating on Clacton beach (the Yorkshire Pierrots, the Jolly Coons and Claude North's Marionettes), a bandstand where regular band concerts were held and an open-air theatre at the West Cliff Gardens as well as two other theatres (the Pier Pavilion and the Operetta House). In 1906 Clacton's 'crowning glory' was opened along Marine Parade West – the Palace-by-the-Sea. Built at a cost of £50,000, it covered an extensive area to the west of the Tower Road martello tower, and its grounds contained many attractions such as a theatre, a bandstand, restaurants, and an illuminated electric fountain plus attractions from around the world, including a Neapolitan Pergola, Blue Caves of Capri and a Japanese Pagoda. The cinema arrived in 1911 with the conversion of the Operetta House into a 'picture palace', while a purpose-built cinema, the Kinema Grand, was opened in 1913.

By the outbreak of the First World War, Clacton had become one of the leading seaside places in the country and, although the war temporarily interrupted this progression, the arrival of the 1920s was to see Clacton continue its march into the very top league of British holiday resorts.

Clacton's post-war fortunes were initially very much bound up with the development of the pier. Peter Bruff's original pier had been enlarged several times between its opening and 1921, with the Pier Pavilion being added in 1893. But its main purpose in life was still as a landing stage for the paddle steamers to disgorge their holiday-makers, both long stay and day trippers. However, the First World War and the increase in rail and road travel had both taken their toll on the pier and the company which owned it went into liquidation. It was at this point that a man called Ernest Kingsman stepped into the picture. He approached the liquidator with a view to purchasing the pier as he was convinced that, with a little capital and a lot of energy, Clacton pier could be made to pay its way. So in 1922 he, his wife and son, Barney, formed the Clacton Pier Company and took over the pier.

Kingsman's judgement that he could turn the pier into a successful entertainment centre seemed to be confirmed when a shy young man approached him and asked if he could have a job entertaining children. The man called himself Clown Bertram and was given a week's trial. The following afternoon Kingsman watched Bertram's first children's show and, in an interview given some years later to *Tit Bits* magazine, Kingsman recalled, 'At the end of the pier a thousand people were standing, and scores of children sitting on the carpet, and they were shrieking with laughter ...'. Ernest Kingsman had confirmation that his conviction was correct and that the future of the pier lay in entertainments. Between 1922 and 1934 he spent about £200,000 on the pier, building three theatres, the Blue Lagoon Dance Hall, a zoo, a funfair, a restaurant, the Crystal Casino amusements and the first open-air pier swimming pool in the country. By the outbreak of war even more entertainments had been added, including a large roller coaster known as the Steel Stella.

By the 1930s Clacton Pier, affectionately known as No.1 North Sea, had become the most utilised pier in the country and was undoubtedly a major factor in the rise of Clacton to the premier division of British seaside resorts, to be spoken of in the same breath as Blackpool, Brighton or Bournemouth.

Along with the pier, the town's amusement and entertainment facilities were growing apace to cater for the ever-increasing number of holiday-makers. At the other end of Clacton another small pier, known as the Jetty, was also being turned into a pleasure pier. This had been built originally as a purely functional landing stage for the barges bringing building materials for the new town. It had never been very successful, but, as part of the West Clacton Estate, it too provided various amusements in the inter-war years including amusement arcades, open-air shows and cafés. The West Clacton Estate itself provided a miniature golf course, boating lakes and, a sign of the times, plenty of car parking space.

During the '20s and '30s the town witnessed a large increase in the number of theatres and cinemas as the open-air pierrot shows and concert parties for the most part gave way to indoor shows. The West Cliff Theatre was built in 1928 on the site of the old West Cliff Gardens open-air stage. The Princes Theatre was opened in 1931 as part of the new Town Hall complex, while the Palace Theatre survived the closure of the Palace-by-the-Sea pleasure grounds.

By the late 1930s there were no less than six cinemas operating simultaneously in Clacton. As well as the Operetta House (renamed the Tivoli in 1924) and the Kinema Grand already mentioned, there was the Palace, converted from the Palace Theatre, the Electric Theatre, opened in Great Clacton in August 1922, the Odeon, opened on 30 May 1936, and the Century, opened on 25 July 1936.

In 1936 the old bandstand in the Pavilion, originally removed there in 1914 from its spot on Marine Parade, was taken away and replaced by a new stage and auditorium behind a glass sea-facing façade. Other entertainments included Marshall's Amusement Arcade opened in 1932 on the site of the old *Brunswick Hotel* in Pier Avenue, the pleasure boats plying for hire off the beach and the regular weekly fête held at the John Groom Orphanage in Old Road. The highlight of this was the 'Orphanage on Fire' display which took place in the evening; flames and smoke appeared at the windows and girls were dramatically rescued by the Staff Fire Brigade. The Vista Road Recreation Ground was opened in 1929 and, from 1931, Essex played county cricket there for one week each season. There was also the Clacton Carnival, which began in 1922 originally as a fund-raising event for Clacton hospital (organised by Ernest Kingsman). This became a regular annual occasion and included a Procession of Decorated Vehicles and Floats and a number of aquatic events.

Finally, in 1937, Butlin's arrived. Billy Butlin had bought the West Clacton Estate in 1936 and by Easter 1937 was ready to open his Pleasure Park on the site. This included many fairground rides (the largest big wheel in the country), side shows, freak shows, speciality and novelty acts, including Dare-Devil Peggy, a one-legged diver, and the Stratosphere Girl, a teenager who performed extraordinary stunts perched on a two-inch wide platform on top of a steel pole 137-ft. high. When the holiday camp itself opened in 1938 it provided further entertainments, with stage shows and sporting events often open to visitors as well as campers.

By the outbreak of the Second World War, Clacton had found its niche as one of the country's leading resorts. Most of its economy and employment depended upon the holiday trade. It provided holidays for 100,000 visitors per week during the summer and was one of the most popular holiday destinations for Londoners, particularly East Londoners, and for those from places in the Midlands which had a direct rail link.

The railway had, in fact, played a very significant role in the continued popularity of Clacton. As the paddle steamer trade declined, Clacton was able to cash in both on its proximity to London (only 70 miles or little more than one and a half hours from Liverpool Street) and on its direct line to Cambridge and the Midlands, with a regular Saturday service to Leicester and Birmingham.

The increasing number of travellers taking to the roads, whether in private car or charabanc, was also well catered for, with the main A12 arterial taking visitors from the heart of London to within a few miles of Clacton. An even bigger boost was provided in 1933 when the Colchester by-pass was opened, built almost exclusively to cope with Clacton's growing holiday trade.

The beach provided two miles of golden sand, with well-kept gardens on the cliff top. Although on the east coast, Clacton has a south-facing prospect which meant that it gained a reputation for long hours of warm sunshine, thus giving rise to its sobriquet 'Sunny Clacton'.

The town itself was always kept clean and the main tree-lined shopping streets provided all the holiday-maker could desire. The big chain stores moved into Clacton – shops such as Woolworth's, W. H. Smith, Marks & Spencer all arrived between the wars. There were also many well-known local shops, such as Grimwade & Clarke's, E. H. Newson & Sons and Gilders & Brown, first-class restaurants, such as Foyster's, Bohemian Café, the Geisha, Prince's, and innumerable hotels, guesthouses and boarding houses.

For that 20-year period Clacton was on top of the world as an active, bustling seaside town with a civic pride and sense of achievement. There was also a sense of knowing what it was doing and where it was going. It was during this period too that Clacton began to expand rapidly in all directions, spreading both east and west along the coast as well as inland. To the east was the ancient village of Little Holland. As recently as 1891 its population had stood at just 78 and, although some building activity had taken place in the early years of the 20th century, by 1911 its population was still only one hundred and seventeen. In 1934, however, Little Holland (renamed Holland-on-Sea) was absorbed into Clacton Urban District. A dual sewerage system was provided, tree-lined roads and promenades were built and rapid expansion took place. Holland-on-Sea nevertheless remained a much quieter suburb for those seeking a more restful holiday or, indeed, a restful retirement.

To the west a completely new development took place in the 1920s and '30s when Frank Stedman bought the old farm of Jaywick and laid out the land for housing development. In spite of considerable opposition from Clacton Urban District Council, who felt the land unsuitable for such development, Stedman was able to build up Jaywick into a small seaside suburb of Clacton. The housing, for the most part, was only supposed to be used for holiday accommodaton, but many people made their homes in the bungalows and chalets of Old Town, Brooklands and Grasslands as the three laid-out areas became known. Only the Tudor Estate was actually designed as a year-round housing estate. Jaywick became a lively small resort in its own right with amusement arcades, donkey rides and typical seaside shops and cafés.

Further inland Clacton was pushing back its boundaries at a rapid rate. The small hamlets of Magdalen Green and Rush Green were early casualties of Clacton's forward march and before long the new town of Clacton-on-Sea had completely engulfed the ancient village of Great Clacton. The major expansion started in the 1930s with Mr. Renshaw's development of Burrsville to the north of Great Clacton. Council house building also took place on the London Road, Elm Grove, Croft and Warwick Road Estates.

Clacton's population continued to grow rapidly during the inter-war years. In 1911 it had stood at just under 10,000, but by the outbreak of the Second World War this had more than doubled. The rise was due partly to the increase in employment opportunities afforded by the expansion of the holiday industry and partly by commuters from both Colchester and London who found life by the seaside more agreeable than town life and stayed.

On 4 June 1939, just before the outbreak of war, there was a major fire in Clacton, which resulted in the complete destruction of the Public Hall, together with a number of the town centre shops such as Lewellens, International Stores, Bohemian Café, Noble the Tobacconist and Baxfield's. With the benefit of hindsight, the fire seems somehow to have been a symbolic end to Clacton's golden era and things were never quite the same again.

When war came, after an initial period of quiet when evacuees were actually sent to Clacton, the town came to resemble a front line military town. The evacuees were sent elsewhere and Clacton's children themselves were evacuated. All persons having no business in the town were sent away and strict regulations were enforced as to who was allowed entry. The population fell to about five thousand.

At first Butlin's was turned into a prisoner-of-war and internees camp, but, as there proved to be not many of either, it was subsequently taken over by the army and used as an army camp. More army personnel were billeted throughout Clacton and the sea front was used for anti-aircraft practice. Other war precautions included the removal of a section of the pier and the complete demolition of the Jetty, while the beaches were mined and fortified with barbed wire and tank traps. Six large trench shelters and 103 brick surface shelters, with a capacity for 3,808 persons, were set up in readiness.

Early in the war, the British press focused its attention on Clacton when a German Heinkel on a land-mine laying mission was shot down and crashed into a row of houses in Victoria Road. Two of the inhabitants were killed and became the first civilian casualties of the war anywhere on mainland Britain.

Altogether there were 1,084 air raid alerts and much damage was done to the town centre, particularly round the old Town Hall and Wagstaff's Corner, Electric Parade and to Bryan's Garage. The war zone restrictions were finally lifted in 1944 and, by 1945, Clacton was once again ready to take up with hope where it had left off in 1939.

However, it was not to be. Although the late 1940s and '50s once again showed Clacton to be a very popular holiday resort there were the first signs of the decline that was to set in more rapidly in the '60s and accelerate through the '70s and '80s.

For a start two of Clacton's largest hotels closed just after the war. *The Towers*, at one time headquarters of the golf club and boasting its own tennis courts, croquet lawns, putting course, bowling green and genuine Burroughs & Watts billiard table, never re-opened after the war. The *Grand*, an A.A. and R.A.C. four-star hotel, struggled on for a couple of seasons but by 1949 was incorporated with *The Towers* in the St Osyth's Teacher Training College. The *East Essex Gazette* noted that: 'for the best sites on the Marine Parade to be occupied by a training college is an economic disaster'.

Only three of the six cinemas re-opened for business after the war, although both the Tivoli (as the Savoy) and the Palace reverted to theatres. On the pier the Children's Theatre and the Crystal Casino had also disappeared for good.

The closure of *The Towers* and the *Grand* was evidence of a shift in emphasis on the type of holiday enjoyed by millions of Britons after the war, for although the big hotels were closing, Butlin's was thriving and actually expanding. But the more affluent '60s were to prove the real turning point for both Butlin's and Clacton. Holiday habits continued to change rapidly with more and more families going abroad. Resorts like Clacton found it very hard to keep going on the same scale as in the pre-war years. Bookings in all hotels and guesthouses dropped alarmingly – other large hotels joined the *Towers* and the *Grand* on the 'closed' list, including *Beaumont Hall*, the *Hadleigh*, *Oulton Hall* and *Grosvenor Court* (damaged by fire in 1963 and never re-opened).

Butlin's went through a bad patch as family bookings dried up and the camp was taken over by groups of single teenagers. During this period the camp earned itself a very poor reputation with stories of all-night parties, chalet swapping, drunkenness and so on, which had the effect of discouraging even more families from staying there. Perhaps the biggest blow of all came at Easter 1964 with the infamous 'Mods' and 'Rockers' riot. Clacton hit the nation's headlines when hordes of teenagers fought running battles with each other and the police. They caused untold damage and drove ordinary people off the streets. Clacton's bookings for that summer plummeted as many families cancelled.

Throughout the 1960s and '70s more and more entertainments closed so that by 1980 just two theatres remained, and only one of those, the West Cliff, put on a summer season. There were only two cinemas, one of which closed in the early 1980s. Most of the attractions on the pier had disappeared, the band pavilion no longer hosted band concerts, Essex had played its last county cricket match at Vista Road in 1966 and the pleasure boat trips were just about to come to an end.

The town itself continued to grow as commuters settled and people retired to the seaside. There was also an expansion of light industry, taking the place of the holiday trade as the main provider of work. Industrial estates at such places as Gorse Lane, Oxford Road and Ford Road continued to thrive. However, when the recession of the early 1980s came, many of these jobs were lost and Clacton became the unemployment black spot of the south-east.

The final blow to Clacton's lingering image as one of the country's leading seaside resorts came in 1983 with the closure of Butlin's and its replacement by a housing estate.

As we approach the mid-1990s, Clacton has settled down to become a fairly quiet seaside resort. It still provides a degree of entertainment for holiday-makers and residents alike. There is still one cinema (the Century) with two screens, and two theatres (the West Cliff and the Princes) are still going strong. The lower part of Pier Avenue is still full of amusement arcades, while Marshall's Amusements has become Magic City, an indoor entertainment centre for children. Vista Road Recreation Ground has expanded and provides much in the way of sporting facilities. The pier's fortunes have revived in recent years and it is still one of the most utilised piers in the country. There are still the beautifully laid-out gardens behind the two miles of golden sand, and Peter Bruff's original plan for the centre of Clacton still provides a shopping centre with wide streets and a feeling of light and space.

As a resort, Clacton's main attraction now is for the day or weekend tripper rather than the long stay holiday-maker. It is nearly one hundred and twenty-five years since the *Queen of the Orwell* landed at Clacton pier and initiated a period of great change. The photographs in this book will bring back memories of those changing times for those that have lived through some of them and give some idea to newer residents and visitors of the Clacton of days gone by.

The Town

1. Clacton's founding father, Peter Bruff, in old age.

2. Clacton's first town hall was built in 1894 on the corner of Rosemary Road, High Street and Station Road. The building originally comprised Barclay's Bank downstairs, the council offices upstairs, with the Operetta House at the back.

3. Those were the days! A 'Pot of Tea, Roll and Butter for one 5d'. This is a view of Station Road looking towards the Town Hall c.1914. The café in question was A. Mazzoleni's at no.31. The photograph was taken by H. Batty, photographer, from his shop next door at no.29.

4. An Edwardian view of Station Road looking north from its junction with Pier Avenue. Originally called North Avenue, its name was changed after the arrival of the railway which terminated near the far end of the road. On the right-hand corner is Thorogood's baker's shop, originally built in the early 1870s for Shadrach Sparling to serve as the town's first post office.

5. A closer view of the left-hand corner of Station Road's junction with Pier Avenue in 1903, showing Grimwade & Clarke, tailors and outfitters, on the spot they were to occupy for over eighty years until finally closing and being demolished in 1984 to make way for McDonald's restaurant.

6. An early view of Electric Parade, so-called because it was the first part of Clacton to be lit by electric light. On the left of this photograph is Newson's Outfitters. This is the only shop in Electric Parade still operating under its original name. The present owner, Brian Newson, is the grandson of the original owner, Ernest Newson.

7. The Rosemary Road end of Electric Parade in 1950, shortly before the road layout was re-designed. Canler & Leighton, the shop in the centre, was one of Clacton's earliest building firms.

8. The other end of Electric Parade about ten years later. It was about this time that the name Electric Parade fell into disuse, although the service road behind the shops is still known today as Back Electric Parade. Grimwade & Clarke's can just be seen on the right. Cook & Eaves is the shop selling Player's Airmen.

9. The lower end of Pier Avenue, c.1912. The large building on the left in the centre was the old Public Hall, built by Bruff and the Woolwich Steam Packet Co. directors in 1877. It was later incorporated into Lewellen's ironmongery shop. On the right is A. Mazzoleni's other café (see Plate 3).

10. Pier Avenue in the late Victorian era showing some of Clacton-on-Sea's earliest buildings dating from the 1870s. Although the right-hand side of the road was destroyed by fire in 1939, all the buildings on the left are still standing, albeit almost unrecognisable behind their modern amusement arcade frontages.

11. By the 1920s Clacton had become a very busy seaside town, as this view of the Pier Avenue/Marine Parade corner shows. On the right is the *Royal Hotel* built by Clacton's pioneers in 1872.

12. Pier Gap originally contained shops on both sides, as this view from the 1890s demonstrates. However, in 1914 the council decided to put into effect a 'general beautifying programme' and demolished all the shops.

13. In their place the council built the Venetian Bridge and landscaped the sides of Pier Gap with rock gardens.

14. A 1938 view of Marine Parade and Pier Gap showing, in the centre, the green-roofed kiosk which is still there today, having survived about sixty years on this site.

15. Marine Parade in the 1950s with the Eastern National open-top summer service bus wending its way to Jaywick.

16. The High Street in the early 1950s, in the days when Barclay's Bank occupied both corners.

17. This view of the High Street does not quite conjure up the image of 'Sunny Clacton', having been taken in the severe winter of 1955. The post office is on the right.

18. London Road under construction in the early 1920s. It was built to provide holiday traffic with a direct route into Clacton, thereby avoiding the village of Great Clacton.

19. One of Clacton's 103 brick-built surface air-raid shelters. This was one in Coppins Road.

20. Another wartime view, this time of the town yard in Old Road, showing the newly-constructed static water tank capable of holding 250,000 gallons of water for 'fire purposes'. Beyond the tank are the gas-works and the old water tower.

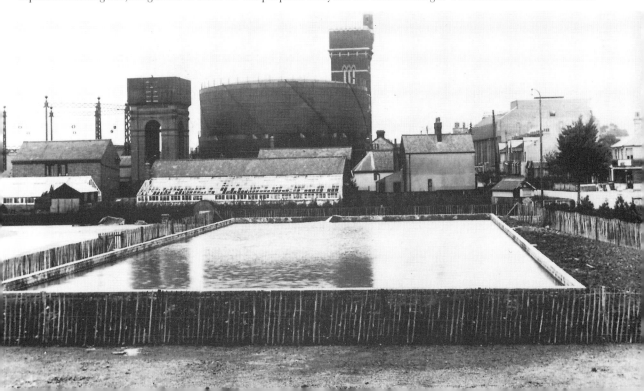

21. St John's church, the centre of village life for centuries. Built in the early 12th century by Richard de Belmeis, Bishop of London, it is now in a poor state of repair and no longer in use.

22. An early 20th-century view of the *Ship Inn* and Brook Street (as Old Road was then known). The *Ship* dates back to the early 16th century and is probably Clacton's second oldest building after the church. The cottages on the right, which included Revell's grocery shop, were destroyed by a fire in 1921.

23. A peaceful scene at the *Queen's Head* at about the turn of the century. The frenetic building then taking place at the seaside had still not caught up with the old village. Mr. Pigg, the owner of the *Queen's Head*, is the rather lage gentleman in the middle of the three standing on the left.

24.   A post-war scene shows Great Clacton still as a mostly undisturbed village. The large barn-like building on the right was originally a maltings belonging to the *Queen's Head*. It is now the site of Gibbs' chemist shop.

25.   At one time, in the 18th and early 19th centuries, this was Clacton's main shopping centre. These houses comprised a grocer's, a draper's, an ironmonger's and a baker's. They were demolished in the mid-1960s. The house at the far end, St John's House, was built *c.*1800 and still survives.

26.   A close-up of Mr. Arthur Ellis's ironmongery store in 1920. This is the shop under the middle window in the previous plate. Arthur Ellis was born in London and came to Clacton with the Essex Cycle Brigade during the First World War. After the war he opened his ironmongery which he called Francis Ellis, an amalgamation of his wife's maiden name and his own.

27. Great Clacton's windmill quickly fell into disuse after its owner, Mr. Charles Beckwith, built a steam mill in 1867. It stood in what is now Windmill Park (hence the name) and was demolished in 1918.

28. A very rural looking Valley Road in the 1930s. The junction with Oxford Road, which can just be seen in the middle distance, is now so busy it needs a roundabout. The cottage in the foreground was called Bull Hill Cottage and was demolished in the late 1950s.

Holland and Jaywick

29.   For many years Little Holland was a very small village outside the Clacton Urban District area. The Stewart family from London, seen here, took camping holidays every year from 1909 to 1914 on land which now constitutes part of Lyndhurst Road.

30.   As late as the 1920s, Holland was still very rural. Apart from A. G. White's garage on the left and Orwell Dairies on the corner of Coronation Road (now Windermere Road), the main road from Clacton to Holland contained very few signs of human habitation.

31. York Road, c.1920. The house in the foreground was called Arcady. Built about 1910, it was one of the oldest houses in what was later to become Holland-on-Sea. Owned originally by Mrs. A. Garner-Watts, it was subsequently bought by Walter Johnson, one of those mainly responsible for building up the seaside resort in the 1930s.

32. Even as late as 1950, the approximate date of this photograph, there were still signs of furrows in the grass, giving an indication of Holland's recent past as farmland.

33. By the 1950s Holland-on-Sea had become a popular seaside resort for those wishing for a quieter time than that offered by the bustling town of Clacton.

34. At one time Holland possessed its own small theatre, the Queen's Hall in King's Road, built by Walter Johnson and seating between about 250 and 300 people. It lasted from 1936 to 1972.

35. Jaywick's first beach hut, on sale in 1930 for £50. At first the authorities were very reluctant to recognise the new estates at Brooklands and Grasslands as Clacton Urban District Council thought the marshy land unsuitable for building permanent dwellings.

36. The only part of Jaywick Sands considered suitable for building by the council was the more upmarket Tudor Estate. This is a photograph of Frank Stedman's estate office for the Tudor Estate, *c*.1936.

JAYWICK SANDS ESTATE

FACING FULL SOUTH

CLACTON-ON-SEA   Phone : CLACTON 497

ROOF PLAN

TYPE No. 3 - - £49 : 10 : 0

PLOTS Now have MAIN DRAINAGE, GAS, WATER and ELECTRIC LIGHT, prices from **£45**

BUNGALOWS from **£50** to **£350**

ALL PLOTS HAVE FRONTAGE TO A CONCRETE ROAD
BUSES TO AND FROM CLACTON EVERY **20** MINUTES

WRITE RESIDENT AGENT : D. L. STEDMAN

37. An advertisement taken from the 1933 *Clacton Guide Book* for one of the chalets available on the Brooklands and Grasslands Estates. The whole of these two areas of Jaywick consisted of these holiday-type chalets and bungalows.

38. To combat the lack of support from official bodies, the Jaywick Sands Freeholders Association was formed in 1931 and held its first meeting in the Jaywick Beach Café, pictured here at about that time. It immediately pressed for the council to lay on electricity and for the post office to deliver letters to individual houses instead of the estate office.

39. In spite of official indifference Jaywick Sands continued to grow throughout the 1930s and the small town began to take on an informal holiday camp atmosphere. This is a view of Brooklands in 1938.

40. By the 1950s the popularity of Jaywick as a small seaside resort had been firmly established. This photograph shows a typical summer Saturday morning with traffic arriving and departing on Golf Green Road, the main road into the resort.

41. This is what the holiday-makers would have found when they got there, a lively beach complete with donkeys.

42. *(right)* Frank Stedman was the brains behind the Jaywick Miniature Railway, which ran from Jaywick Sands station to Crossways station (shown here). It operated from 1936 until the outbreak of war and was an extremely popular attraction.

43. *(below)* Jaywick's main problem has always been its low-lying position and it has had to fight a continuous battle with the sea. These defences were erected in early 1950 along the Brooklands front.

44. *(below right)* The fight has not always been successful. Bad floods occurred in 1936, 1949 and, of course, 1953 when 35 people lost their lives in the devastation wrought on the night of 31 January/1 February.

CHALETS
TO LET

Shops and Businesses

45.   Henry Foyster opened his dining and tea rooms in Pier Avenue in the 1890s.

46. Looking out from Foyster's tea rooms in the 1930s. The tea rooms lasted until well after the Second World War.

47. Henry Foyster had two other shops, one in Rosemary Road and this one on the other side of Pier Avenue, next to the *Brunswick Hotel*, now Magic City.

48. The West Clacton Laundry was established in St Osyth Road in 1899 and was run for many years by the Davall family. In 1900 it advertised that it was open for public inspection on Wednesdays and Thursdays 'when intending patrons may satisfy themselves of the careful methods adopted'.

49. Abraham Quick & Co. Ltd. were for many years Clacton's leading printers, being responsible for, amongst other things, the local newspapers *Clacton News* and *East Essex Gazette*. This is their establishment in Station Road in the late 1890s.

50. W. E. Thorogood established his bakery in Oxford Road in 1896. According to the 1900 *Clacton Guide* it was the 'finest of its kind in East Anglia'. His shop was on the corner of Station Road and Pallister Road (see Plate 4).

51.   An 1897 view of the pair of houses on the corner of Rosemary Road and The Grove. In 1901 the ground floors were converted into a parade of shops. Unfortunately, this was the same year as Electric Parade opened and the venture suffered financially as a result. Behind the shops the same buildings still occupy the corner today, although the rural setting has long since disappeared.

52.   Clacton's postmen line up outside the post office in 1907. The post office was opened in 1901 at 9 Electric Parade and remained there until 1927, when it moved to its present building in the High Street. No.9 Electric Parade is now occupied by W. H. Smith & Sons Ltd.

53. The International Stores' bacon counter during the Edwardian era. International Stores had two shops in Clacton: this one in Station Road, opened around the turn of the century, and another in Pier Avenue, which was destroyed in the 1939 Lewellen's fire.

54. Johnson's in Rosemary Road won first prize in the Clacton Chamber of Commerce's 'Shop Window Dressing Competition' in 1920 with this window. Johnson's is Clacton's longest established grocer's shop.

55. Arthur Fitch started his general engineering and smithy business in Rosemary Road in 1880. He and his son, Frank, drifted into the motor business and even ran a bus service, the Enterprise, in the 1920s. In 1934 Fitch Motors also bought the old Lifeboat House in Carnarvon Road (seen here) in order to extend their business.

56. This photograph, dating from about 1936/7, shows a Fitch advertising car. The cars were a common sight around Clacton and the business lasted until well after the Second World War.

57 & 58.   For many years, until nationalisation in the late 1940s, Clacton Urban District Council had the responsibility for providing Clacton with its gas and electricity services. These are two adverts from the 1933 *Clacton Guide Book*.

59.   In its heyday Clacton could boast many large hotels all along and just off the sea front. A typical example was the *Grosvenor Court Hotel* at 35 and 37 Marine Parade East. Opened just after the First World War, it was destroyed by fire in 1963.

Transport

60. *(above)* Practically the only way of reaching Clacton in its early years as a seaside resort was by sea. There was no railway and the roads were very poor. The Belle Steamers operated on the route from London from 1890 until the 1930s, and are seen here, *c*.1904.

61. *(above right)* Although increasingly challenged by road and rail over the years, paddle steamers retained some of their popularity until the Second World War. This is one of the most famous, the *Golden Eagle*, disgorging passengers at the pier head in the mid-1930s. Also taking on trippers is a small pleasure boat, the *Gay Commodore*.

62. *(right)* The popularity of steamers declined sharply after the war. For a while during the 1950s, the *Queen of the Channel* continued to operate services to London, as well as running day trips to France, but the days of regular runs from London to Clacton were numbered.

63. For many years the 'Claud Hamilton' 4-4-0, designed by James Holden, was the mainstay of the London-Clacton line. No.1870, the engine pictured here leaving Clacton station, was built in 1902. Before being allocated to the Clacton line it had been used to pull King Edward VII's train from Liverpool Street to Sandringham. This photograph was taken some time after the Great Eastern Railway had merged with a number of other companies to form the L.N.E.R. in 1923.

64. The Essex Coast Express at the end of its inaugural run on 9 June 1958. Hauled by Britannia Pacific-type locomotives, the service succeeded in reducing the scheduled journey time from London to Clacton to 86 minutes. This is No.70000, 'Britannia'.

65. Three wagonettes line up in Old Road (opposite Green Lodge) for an outing just before the First World War.

66. With improvements to the roads, such as the London Road (Plate 18) and the Colchester by-pass, in the 1920s and '30s, the charabanc became a very popular method of transport for the works, pub or club outing to Clacton, rivalling the train and the paddle steamer. Here is one such outing pictured outside Foyster's restaurant in the mid-1920s.

67. Clacton's first motor coach company was Barnes Coaches. The owner was Mr. Chas Barnes, the first person in Clacton to be issued with a '(Public) Drivers Licence'. His first coach, seen here shortly after its maiden run on 14 August 1906 from Clacton to St Osyth, was called the Swiftsure, but, owing to its unreliability, was nicknamed the 'Neversure' by locals.

68. The Swiftsure's programme of drives, c.1908.

69. Mr. Barnes continued in business after the First World War with a long succession of coaches all called 'Progress'. Barnes Coaches finally went out of business in 1987.

70. Chas Barnes in his days as a London tramcar driver before coming to Clacton.

71. Clacton & District Motor Services was founded in 1913 by Mr. W. P. Allen. The fleet name was changed to 'Silver Queen' in 1926 and was acquired by Eastern National in 1931. During the 1920s the Silver Queen was Clacton's major bus service operating as far afield as Harwich, Brightlingsea and Colchester.

72. In the 1950s many coach companies were providing regular daily or weekly services to Clacton including Sutton's, Grey Green, Empire's Best and the one pictured here in its Warwick Castle coach station, Premier Travel. Premier Travel ran a regular service from Clacton to Birmingham and Coventry with connecting services to Manchester and Preston.

73. The Laking biplane made its maiden flight at Clacton on 4 July 1911, which probably means it was the first aeroplane ever to fly over Clacton. Designed by Guy Laking, it was built by Frank Fitch in a specially erected garage at Bocking's Elm. The pilot was Anthony Westlake.

74. In the 1930s, Hillman's Airways operated a regular daily service from their aerodrome at Alton Park to Romford.

75.   Frank Fitch continued his plane-making activities until the 1930s when he constructed his own version of the famous French 'kit plane', the 'Flying Flea', at his garage in Carnarvon Road (the old Lifeboat House – see Plate 55).

76.   Much of the building material for the new town of Clacton-on-Sea was brought from Colchester and Ipswich by barge. In 1898 a jetty was constructed for these barges, but, as can be seen in this picture, the barge owners preferred to run their barges up on to the beach, unload and then wait for high tide to float off again.

77.   Clacton's first lifeboat, the *Albert Edward*, was launched in 1878. This photograph shows Clacton's fourth lifeboat, the *Edward Z Dresden*, launched in March 1929 and finally taken out of service in January 1952 after taking part in 181 rescues and saving 112 lives.

78.　Clacton's first motorised fire engine, a Merryweather, was introduced following criticism of the fire brigade's slow response to the fire on 24 June 1921 which destroyed Petley's hairdressing salon in Pier Avenue. Although the fire brigade denied it, witnesses said there had been a delay in catching the horses to pull the old fire engine!

79. Zach Fairclough stands next to one of his fleet of five steam rollers, the 'Clacton Belle', a Garrett 10-ton single cylinder, driven here by Jack Faiers. Prior to the purchase of their own steamroller, Zach carried out all Clacton Council's road rolling work. He also owned numerous landaus, wagonettes and phaetons and later started a charabanc business and ran a removal service. In the 1920s he was Clacton's highest payer of rates, owning nearly one hundred houses, which he rented out. By the time of his death in 1933 he was a very wealthy man, but was still unable to read or write!

The Beach

80. This engraving appeared in a *The Times* in July 1871 to commemorate the opening of the pier and is therefore the earliest known pictorial representation of Clacton-on-Sea.

81. Some thirty years on, a view of the same section of Clacton beach.

82. A view of the busy beach west of the pier in 1903. On the left the Yorkshire Pierrots, in the centre Batty the 'People's Photographer' and on the right the covered slope of the Reno Electric Stairway, an escalator constructed in 1902 to convey passengers up the cliff face.

83. The Reno Electric Stairway was a failure as people preferred to walk up the cliff face instead of paying the 1d. required to ride. In 1908 the escalator was removed and in 1909 the council agreed to construct the path seen in this photograph. Batty, the photographer, had also moved to the jetty.

84.   From his new kiosk on the jetty, Mr. Batty would emerge every so often and blow a whistle. At this signal, everyone who wanted their photo taken would line up and 'watch the birdie'. Later in the day the photograph was put on sale in his tent for 6d. This photograph was the result of one such session.

85. After its failure as a landing stage (see Plate 76), Clacton jetty became a small pleasure pier in the 1920s and '30s. It was demolished in 1940 as a wartime precaution.

86. The pleasure boat in the centre is the *Viking Saga*, while the *Nemo II* is the one taking aboard trippers on the beach. Clacton beach was still very popular as a seaside resort in the 1950s.

87.   The St John's ambulance parked outside the Pavilion during the summer ready to pick up any casualties from the beach. From left to right are: Mr. D. Pendrill, Miss Norton, Mr. Brinkman and Mrs. G. Agate.

88.   By the 1950s all the pierrot and concert party stands had disappeared, but the Salvation Army held regular services and gospel 'sing-songs' on the beach.

The Pier

89. The pier, *c*.1922, just about the time it was bought by the Kingsman family.

90 & 91. Ernest and Ada Kingsman and their son, Barney. The Kingsmans owned the pier for almost 50 years and between them they played a major part in Clacton's role as a leading seaside resort.

92. By 1926, the date of this photograph, the Kingsmans had already built the first Blue Lagoon Dance Hall on the left of the pier entrance, the Children's Theatre and introduced Skeeball. This was a game which consisted of bowling a ball up a slope in which there were numbered holes. The ball dropped through the holes and high scores were awarded with tokens which could then be exchanged for a prize.

93. The holiday crowds enjoy some of the pier's new amusements, c.1930.

94. Another major pier attraction in the 1930s was the newly-introduced dodgems, brought to this country from America by Billy Butlin.

95.   The pier, *c*.1934, now reaping the rewards of its £200,000 investment with huge crowds visiting its many new attractions.

96. Professor Webb used to perform diving stunts off the pier throughout the Edwardian period. On one occasion, however, one of his most famous stunts, that of diving in with a lighted cigarette and coming up with it still lit, ended in disaster for the professor when, on surfacing, his false teeth shot out and were lost forever beneath the waves!

97. By far the most popular performer ever to appear on the pier was Clown Bertram, here surrounded by his 'Bright Young Things'. Clown Bertram appeared for the entire summer season every year from 1922 until 1939.

98. Originally Bertram performed in the open air with just a handful of seats in front of him. He proved so popular, however, that Ernest Kingsman built him his own theatre, the Children's Theatre, which could seat five hundred. Even this was not big enough and he eventually moved into the 1,000-seat Pier Pavilion. This is a view of a typical queue awaiting his performance.

99. Will C. Pepper's White Coons were popular performers on the pier in the Edwardian and inter-war periods.

100. The Ramblas open air concert party began in the 1930s and continued until 1964, making them one of the last open air concert parties to appear on a regular basis anywhere in the country. The shows were produced by and starred Gordon Henson, who is on the extreme left of this photograph. Another regular, Clare Ruane, is in the centre.

101.   Dancing to Teddy Dobbs and his Band in the Blue Lagoon Dance Hall in the 1930s.

102.   The Steel Stella roller coaster was constructed in 1937. This view shows one of the ride's covered cars arriving on 10 June 1937.

103. By the 1950s the crowds were still coming in large numbers to use the Steel Stella and the Helter Skelter.

104. The Steel Stella in operation in the 1950s, with the children's train to the right and the ghost train to the left. The Steel Stella was destroyed by fire in 1973.

105. Another busy pier scene in the 1950s showing the helter skelter, known as the Cresta Run.

106. The speedboat was yet another popular attraction just after the war, as it still is today. In the middle distance is the Ocean Theatre, opened in 1928 and closed in 1978 after 50 years of attracting the very biggest names in show business, including George Robey, Nellie Wallace and Tony Hancock.

19472

107. An aerial view of the pier
*c.*1950 showing all the
entertainments on the pier.

108. The pier staff in 1925. Clown
Bertram is fifth from the left in the
front row. His dummy, Filbert, is in
the centre of the front row. Ada and
Ernest Kingsman are seventh and
eighth from the left in the row
behind.

Entertainments

109. Harry Frewin's White Coons, later the Jolly Coons, had their stand near the jetty during the Edwardian period.

110. The West Cliff Theatre was built in 1928 on the site of the open air Westcliff Gardens Theatre, founded by Bernard Russell, Bert Graham and Will Bentley, who had first performed on the site in 1894. Many big stars of the '30s appeared at the West Cliff. It is one of only two theatres still open in Clacton.

111. The other theatre to remain open is the Princes Theatre, shown here in the 1950s. Before the war the Princes was home to many visiting professional and local amateur repertory companies.

112. During the Second World War the Princes was used to keep up morale for the many troops stationed in the area. This is a concert taking place in July 1941 called 'The Forces Vo-de-o-do' starring Clare Luce.

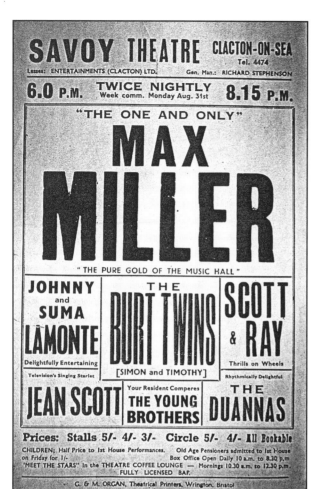

SAVOY THEATRE CLACTON-ON-SEA
Tel. 4474
Lessees: ENTERTAINMENTS (CLACTON) LTD. Gen. Man.: RICHARD STEPHENSON

6.0 P.M. TWICE NIGHTLY **8.15 P.M.**
Week comm. Monday Aug. 31st

"THE ONE AND ONLY"

MAX MILLER

" THE PURE GOLD OF THE MUSIC HALL "

JOHNNY and SUMA LAMONTE	THE BURT TWINS	SCOTT & RAY
Delightfully Entertaining	[SIMON and TIMOTHY]	Thrills on Wheels
Television's Singing Starlet		Rhythmically Delightful

JEAN SCOTT	Your Resident Comperes THE YOUNG BROTHERS	THE DUANNAS

Prices: Stalls 5/- 4/- 3/- Circle 5/- 4/- All Bookable

CHILDREN; Half Price to 1st House Performances.   Old Age Pensioners admitted to 1st House
on Friday for 1/-   Box Office Open Daily 10 a.m. to 8.30 p.m
"MEET THE STARS" in the THEATRE COFFEE LOUNGE — Mornings 10.30 a.m. to 12.30 p.m.
FULLY LICENSED BAR.

G. & M. ORGAN, Theatrical Printers, Wrington, Bristol.

113.   Clacton's other major theatre after the war was the Savoy Theatre, the re-named Operetta House. Again many big names in variety entertainment appeared there including Billy Cotton and Max Miller. The compères for this show were the Young Brothers, Reg and Bob, still, I am pleased to report, going strong today.

114.   Stanley Holloway, pictured here in a scene from the film *The Girl from Maxim's* with Lady Tree, was a regular performer with Graham and Bentley at the West Cliff Gardens from 1912-14, where he was billed as a 'romantic baritone'. He lived in Beatrice Road and Ellis Road and married his first wife, Queenie, in Clacton.

115. *(above)* Frankie Howerd's first ever summer season was at Clacton in a show called 'For the Fun of It', starring Nosmo King, at the West Cliff Theatre in 1947.

116. *(above right)* As a young entertainer, Roy Hudd had a season as a Butlin redcoat at Clacton in 1958. He subsequently starred for two seasons at the Ocean Theatre and has returned many times. Recently he played a major role in raising funds for badly needed structural alterations at the West Cliff Theatre.

117. *(right)* Cliff Richard had his first ever professional engagement in Clacton, at Butlin's in 1958, when he was hired to play in the *Pig & Whistle Bar* and later the South Seas Coffee Bar.

118. One of Clacton's six cinemas, the Electric Theatre in Old Road, Great Clacton. Opened in 1922, it closed at the beginning of the Second World War. The building has now been incorporated into Suswin's clothing factory.

119. A nostalgic view, c.1950, looking along Agate Road towards the Odeon which, in its day, was the last word in luxury cinema and one of the large Odeon chain built all over the country in the 1930s. Opened in 1936, it closed in 1983, by which time it had been renamed the Salon.

120.   The bandstand on Marine Parade East was built in 1899 to accommodate Clacton's resident German band under the direction of George Badger, as well as visiting regimental military bands. It is shown here *c.*1903.

121. In 1914 the bandstand was relocated to the new sunken pavilion next to the pier as part of the council's 'general beautifying programme'. The Pavilion had a glass front facing the sea to protect audiences from the wind.

122. The new band stage and auditorium, built in 1936, was used for many other activities besides band concerts. This is the Evening Standard Fashion Parade held regularly throughout the 1950s.

123. The Ronnie Mills Orchestra was the resident band at the Pavilion for many years. With Harry Thompson, Ronnie Mills also organised the very successful Midnight Holiday Dances with dance bands such as Ted Heath, Mantovani and Ray Connif. Ronnie Mills is standing in the centre of the three at the front of the lorry in this early 1950s photograph.

124. Another popular holiday attraction throughout the '50s and '60s was the 'Ideal Holiday Girl' contest also held at the Band Pavilion. The winner in 1957 was Christinar Griggs. On the left is runner-up Andria Loren, while on the right is third placed Doreen Nicholson.

125. There was also an indoor theatre built as part of the Pavilion complex. In the winter it was given over to indoor bowls, and is shown here in the 1950s. It is now an amusement arcade and café.

126. Along Marine Parade West was the model yacht pond, a favourite with boys of all ages. Behind it was the Palace-by-the-Sea.

127.   This photograph, dating from *c.*1906, depicts Tibet, one of the many attractions from around the world, inside the Palace grounds.

128.   The area now known as Martello Bay has had a very varied history. In the early years of this century it was home to this primitive form of holiday camp.

129.   The 148-acre site was bought by four prominent Clacton businessmen, Frederick Wagstaff, Robert Coan, George Gardiner and Henry Foyster who turned it into an outdoor leisure complex known as the West Clacton Estate.

130.   The West Clacton Estate on Whit Monday 1934. The motor car is clearly beginning to make its presence felt.

131.   Billy Butlin bought the Estate in 1936 and opened his second holiday camp on the site on 11 June 1938. After its closure in 1983, the area was mostly turned over to housing.

132.   A view of Butlin's 'main street' in its halcyon days of the 1950s. The Gaiety Theatre on the right was the home of nightly entertainment; downstairs the foyer contained a cafeteria and lounge. Further along was the *Pig and Whistle* bar where Cliff Richard made his professional debut, and on the left is the Regency building which contained a large dance hall.

THE STRATOSPHERE GIRL
On a Flexible Steel Mast, 137 ft. high in Mid-Air
At BUTLIN'S PLEASURE PARK
CLACTON-ON-SEA
From JULY 24th, 1938
THE SENSATION OF SENSATIONS!

133. *(left)* Camilla Meyer, otherwise known as the Stratosphere Girl, was a regular visitor to both the Butlin's Pleasure Park and the holiday camp before the war. This postcard dates from 1938.

134. *(above)* Len Harvey, at the time British light-heavyweight boxing champion, visited the camp in 1938 and 1939. Here he is being introduced to the campers by Billy Thorburn, leader of Butlin's resident band at the time.

135. *(below)* This 1938 newspaper advertisement gives some idea of the big names appearing at Butlin's. As well as those advertised, the 'Cabaret & Ball' on Friday 8 July included Elsie and Doris Waters, George Robey, Vic Oliver and Hildegaarde.

SUNDAY, JULY 3rd to SATURDAY, JULY 9th

BUTLIN'S

ADMISSION · DAILY 10 a.m. to 6 p.m. — 1/-

LUXURY HOLIDAY CAMP : CLACTON

Festival of holiday, health and happiness
—A WEEK OF WORLD-FAMOUS ATTRACTIONS—

DURING EACH DAY:

OPEN TO THE PUBLIC

EXHIBITION BOXING
by LEN HARVEY, Light-Heavy Weight Champion of Great Britain.

EXHIBITION TENNIS
by DAN MASKELL, Professional Lawn Tennis Champion for 9 consecutive years and F. H. POULSON (Runner-up. 1937)

EXHIBITION SWIMMING & DIVING
by E. H. TEMME, the Channel Swimmer and BRISCOE RAY, the Olympic Diving Champion, also an Exhibition by the Highgate Diving Club.

EXHIBITION TABLE TENNIS
by J. K. HYDE, Swaythling Cup Player and Internationalist 1933-38, and R. D. JONES Swaythling Cup 1930-36.

SNOOKER MATCH
for Purse of 100 Guineas between JOE DAVIS and H. LINDRUM.

Dancing throughout the Week

to

LEW STONE AND HIS BAND

•

MANTOVANI
AND
HIS ORCHESTRA

EVENINGS:

MONDAY, JULY 4th   ALL OPEN TO THE PUBLIC
GRAND BOXING SHOW & FIRST PUBLIC DANCE
Admission 2/6. 8.15—12. Fully Licensed.

TUESDAY, JULY 5th
BALL & AMATEUR NIGHT
Admission 2/6. 8.15—12. Fully Licensed.

WEDNESDAY, JULY 6th
LOCAL CHARITY BALL
In aid of new Operating Table Clacton & District Hospital
Admission 5/- 8.15—12. Fully Licensed.

THURSDAY. JULY 7th.
CARNIVAL NIGHT
Demonstrations by Mr. and Mrs. VICTOR SYLVESTER
Admission 2/6. 8.15—12. Fully Licensed.

FRIDAY. JULY 8th.
BROADCAST 8.15—9 p.m.
CABARET & BALL
Dancing from 9.30—12. Fully Licensed.
Admission 10/6, including Running Buffet.

SATURDAY, JULY 9th
CARNIVAL BALL
In aid of a well-known Theatrical Charity.
3.15—11.45. Admission 2/6. Fully Licensed.

John Groom's Crippleage and Flower Girls Mission,
(INCORPORATED)
London and Clacton-on-Sea.

ORPHAN GIRLS PLAITING THE MAYPOLE.

136. Plaiting the maypole at the John Groom Orphanage's regular weekly fête in the early 1920s.

137. Near the Butlin's Pleasure Park was Clacton's open-air roller-skating rink which reached the height of its popularity in the 1950s.

138.   The Punch and Judy show on the West Beach, run by Claude North Junior, was on the site of his father's 'Living and String Marionettes' stand. The Punch and Judy lasted well into the 1960s.

The Carnival

139.   In the early days of the Carnival, the Clacton Swimming Club played a prominent part in organising the activities. Just exactly what they are organising here, in this photograph from 1926, is not too clear however!

140. The most sought-after prize of Carnival week was the one for the best decorated vehicle in the procession. This is the winning float in the 1937 Carnival, a joint entry from Eastern National Omnibus Co. and the Hebrocliff Guest House called 'Rule Britannia'.

141. The Carnival procession lines up at the Butlin's end of the town ...

142. ... and moves off along Marine Parade West ...

143. ... it then turns into Pier
Avenue opposite the kiosk ...

144.   ... and carries on up Pier Avenue past the Gaiety and Criterion restaurants and Marshall's Amusements ...

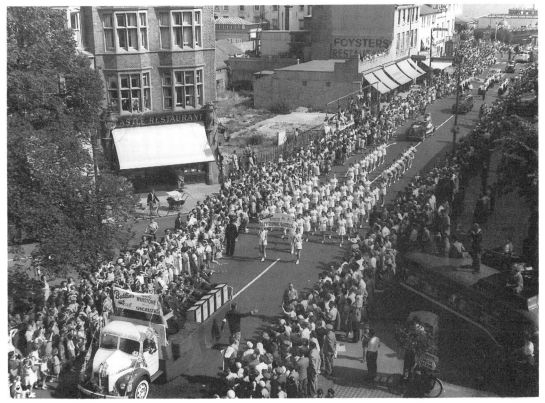

145.   ... before turning into Station Road and eventually back on to Marine Parade to finish up at the Holland end. This photograph, taken of the 1947 procession, shows the derelict land in Pier Avenue following the 1939 fire (see Plates 159-61).

146.   For some reason this procession from the early 1950s seems to be going in the opposite direction. The derelict land next to Foyster's restaurant has now been built upon.

Sport

147. *(right)* Clacton Town Football Club was founded in the 1892/3 season. In 1933 the team was a founder member of the Eastern Counties League. In 1958 they were promoted to the Southern League, dropping back to the Eastern Counties League (now the Jewson League) in 1964. This is a picture of the club at their former ground in Old Road.

148. *(left)* Without a doubt, Clacton's greatest ever footballer was Vivian J. Woodward (1879-1954). He played for Spurs and Chelsea and was capped in 66 internationals for England. He also captained the winning England team in both the 1908 and 1912 Olympic Games. He still holds the record for the most goals scored in one international – seven against France in 1906.

149. *(right)* This is a telegram from Vivian Woodward's brother, Alec, reporting that Jack (as he was known to his family) had scored two goals in his debut international against Ireland at Wolverhampton on 14 February 1903.

POST OFFICE TELEGRAPHS.

No. of Telegram........

Office Stamp.

GLASGOW PE14 02

If the accuracy of an Inland Telegram be doubted, the telegram will be repeated on payment of half the amount originally paid for its transmission, any fraction of 1d. less than ½d. being reckoned as ½d.; and if it be found that there was any inaccuracy, the amount paid for repetition will be refunded. Special conditions are applicable to the repetition of Foreign Telegrams.

| Charges to pay | £ | s. | d. |

Addresses

Handed in at Wolverhampton at 5.1½ M., Received here at 5.3½ M.

TO Dawall Stosyth Rd

Blactononsea

England four Ireland nil Jack

2 Alec

N.B.—This Form must accompany any inquiry made respecting this Telegram.

150. *(left)* A large crowd watching the Essex vs. Leicestershire county cricket match at Vista Road Recreation Ground in 1947.

151. *(below left)* Probably the best performance at Vista Road was Trevor Bailey's 10-90 in one innings against Lancashire in 1949. Bailey is pictured here padded up ready for his innings.

152. *(below)* In 1957 Clacton Cricket Club played a special match against a fathers and sons team. The sons are standing behind their respective fathers, which include V. C. Spurgeon, first on the left, and Arnold Quick, club chairman, third from the left. In one match in 1953, Arnold Quick scored 182 in 62 minutes and then went on to take five wickets.

153.   Clacton has had its fair share of other sporting activity besides football and cricket. For many years Clacton's football stadium in Old Road also doubled as a greyhound stadium as can be seen in this photograph from the late 1960s.

154.   Water polo has also been very popular. This photograph shows a match taking place in the pier swimming pool in the 1930s.

155.   A number of hotels, notably *Beaumont Hall* and this one, the *Towers*, provided their own sporting facilities for guests.

156.   Harry Clarke watches Clacton fire brigade fight a stack fire at Cann Hall Farm in 1906. Harry's brother, William, farmed at Cann Hall for many years.

157.   In September 1904 the War Office decided to test Britain's readiness in case of invasion from Europe, so they organised a mock invasion at Clacton during the summer season. One hundred and fifty thousand troops came ashore amidst holiday-makers, bathing machines, Pierrot shows, the lot. After advancing as far as Witham, the 'invaders' were beaten back to the coast. This photograph shows them re-embarking.

158.   The message on the back of this postcard sent on 30 April 1914 reads: 'This is the aeroplane that put in for repairs. Mr. Winston Churchill spent a few hours at the *Royal Hotel*'. On his return to the new seaplane brought in to take him away, Churchill was barracked by Clacton's branch of the Suffragettes.

159. A parade along Rosemary Road around the time of the First World War, possibly during a recruiting exercise.
It also clearly shows the Operetta House after its conversion into a cinema.

160 & 161. A sign of Clacton's confidence and civic pride in the 1930s, Clacton's Town Hall was opened with great ceremony on 14 April 1931.

CLACTON URBAN DISTRICT COUNCIL

ADMIT   438

TO

TOWN HALL, CLACTON-ON-SEA

ON THE OCCASION OF THE

Opening Ceremony

TUESDAY, 14th APRIL, 1931

Admission only by the Entrance in The Grove

TICKET HOLDERS ARE REQUESTED TO OCCUPY THEIR SEATS BY **12 15** P.M., AFTER WHICH TIME SEATS WILL NOT BE RESERVED

162. The aftermath of a flood in Cambridge Road on 17 September 1934. It was caused by a burst water main. There was no rain that week!

163. Barbara Foyster greets the Hungarian national swimming team at the railway station on its visit to Clacton in 1934. Third from the right wearing a beret is Ernest Kingsman and on his right, holding his hat, is Mr. J. Ball, chairman of the council.

164. The 'Great Fire of Clacton' began in the yard behind Lewellen's shop in Pier Avenue at 3.00 p.m. on Sunday 4 June 1939.

165. Douglas Lewellen looks on helplessly as his shop becomes a raging inferno. The fire was eventually brought under control by the Clacton and Colchester fire brigades at about 6.00 p.m. Hourly bulletins on the progress of the fire were broadcast on B.B.C. radio.

166. The scene of destruction the morning after.

167. The scene in Victoria Road on the morning after the mine-laying Heinkel IIIE had crashed causing the first mainland civilian fatalities of the Second World War.

168. The old town hall was badly damaged by a lone raider in May 1941. The council steamroller in the centre was used to demolish the town clock which had become very unsafe.

People

169. Clacton's fire brigade before November 1904 with Johnnie Fairclough, Zach's son, at the reins. Johnnie was killed in a tragic accident that month when, on hearing the fire bell, he raced bareback on one of the horses to the fire station but was struck by a large branch that was overhanging the road.

170. Clacton's police shortly before the First World War outside their police station in Jackson Road.

171. Clacton's very own company, H Company, in the early days of the First World War. They were attached to the 5th Battalion, Essex regiment. In the back row, first left is William Fairclough, of Clacton's well-known Fairclough family. H Company took part in the Gallipoli landings in August 1915, where William was injured.

172. Sir John Pybus, seen here opening the pier swimming pool in 1932, was M.P. for the Harwich constituency from 1929-35 and was also Minister of Transport. He lived at the Moot Hall on Marine Parade East.

173. Dr. William Gillespie will be well-remembered by Clactonians who lived through the Second World War. As one of the very few doctors left in the town he worked long hours, both in his general practice by day and at Clacton hospital by night where he performed many emergency operations after air raids. He was also Medical Officer to Clacton Town Football Club.

174. Clacton fire brigade's blue watch on duty at Carlton Garage during the Second World War.

175. Clacton's councillors for 1948/9. Included in the line up are: Capt. E. R. Pennel (extreme right, back row), Mr. J. Ball (extreme left) and, in the front row, Mr. H. P. (Percy) King (second from left), Mrs. P. (Florrie) Coleman (third from left), the Chairman Mr. B. Greaves (with chain of office) and Mrs. Lorna Gillespie (seventh from left).

176. The Pathfields School football team with the headmaster, Edward A. ('Jumbo') Read seated in the centre. Pathfields Senior Mixed (now Colbayns) opened in 1931 with Read as its first headmaster. He retired in 1946. Also in this photograph is Frank Saltmarsh (third from the left, back row), a member of the well-known Saltmarsh family, whose general store in St Osyth Road celebrated its centenary in 1992.

177. The Clacton County High School sixth form in 1959. Seated in front is the newly-appointed headmaster, Dr. Gardner, who took up his post on 1 January that year.

178. The pupils at St Osyth Road School during the Edwardian period. Mr. A. E. Brown, the headmaster, is on the extreme right. He was the school's first headmaster, appointed in 1893; he retired in 1920.

179. Mr. Brown's place was taken by Mr. H. W. Learoyd, seen in the centre of this photograph and still well remembered by generations of schoolchildren in Clacton. He was headmaster until 1952, when he transferred with the junior school to Alton Park. He retired in 1953.

180. Nora and Bill Timmens. Bill was Chairman of the Council 1959-60; Nora was born in Clacton in 1903 and was involved in all aspects of Clacton life for all of her 88 years. Her interests included amateur dramatics, the swimming club and the Girl Guides. Her devotion to Clacton earned her an editorial all to herself in the *Gazette*'s special centenary edition.

Bibliography

Allen, C. J., *The Great Eastern Railway*, 1955

Baker, T., *Clacton-on-Sea in Old Picture Postcards*, Vols.1 and 2, 1984 and 1992

Banks, I., *Rails to Jaywick Sands*, 1988

Box, P., *Belles of the East Coast*, 1989

Butlin, Sir B., *The Billy Butlin Story*, 1982

Clacton & District Local History Society, *Town Walk No.1*, 1989

Clacton & District Local History Society, *Newsletter* and *Clacton Chronicle*, 1985-1993

Froom, J., *A Century of Valour*, 1978

Grieve, H., *The Great Tide*, 1959

Hardwick, G., *Paper Clips*, *c.*1990

Jacobs, N., *Clacton in Camera*, 1984

Jacobs, N., *The Sunshine Coast*, 1986

Morris, J., *Story of the Clacton-on-Sea Lifeboats*, 1991

Phillips, C., *The Tendring Hundred Railway*, 1989

Read, S., *Hello Campers*, 1986

Rouse, M., *Coastal Resorts of East Anglia*, 1982

Skudder, J. M., *The Seaside Resort as a Business Venture*, 1985

Walker, K., *The History of Clacton*, 1966

Ward, C., and Hardy, D., *Arcadia for All*, 1984

Ward, C., and Hardy, D., *Goodnight Campers*, 1986

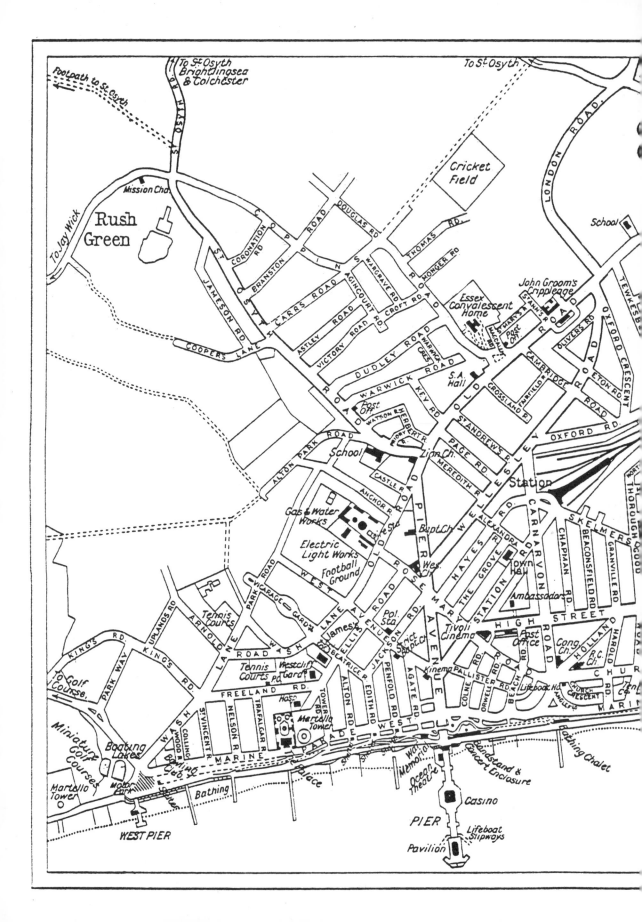